SHIFT HAPPENS: RESTORED TO BLOOM

JILL ROGERS

Copyright © 2019 by Jill Rogers

All rights reserved. No part of this publication may be reproduced, distributed, or transmitted in any form or by any means, including photocopying, recording, or other electronic or mechanical methods, without the prior written permission of the publisher, except in the case of brief quotations embodied in reviews and certain other non-commercial uses permitted by copyright law.

Scripture quotations are taken from: THE HOLY BIBLE, NEW INTERNATIONAL VERSION ® NIV ® Copyright © 1973, 1978, 1984 by International Bible Society ® Used by permission. All rights reserved worldwide

ISBN-13: 978-0-578-60443-5

CONTENTS

Acknowledgments v
Introduction vii

1. From a Seedling — 1
2. As I Understood — 6
3. Seedtime and Harvest — 10
4. Seeds Sown This Year — 14
5. The 12 Steps of Recovery — 16
6. Digging Out Those Roots — 22
7. Sweet Abilene — 28
8. Back to Familiar Soil — 32
9. Top Ten Songs — 38
10. Communion with God Ministries — 42
11. Meditations: Fresh Water and Rain — 46
12. My Cheerleader of Dreams — 50
13. Starting the Day Off Right — 54
14. Weight Watchers — 58
15. 2019: Restored to Bloom — 62
16. "Restored to Bloom" — 66

About the Author 68
Resources 69
Also Available 71

DEDICATION

This book is dedicated to my Heavenly Father that continues to bring me all the fresh new things that water and nourish me, so that I can sow the seeds to others.

To my husband Marty who believes in me and walks alongside me as we carry out this mission

My ancestors that made me who I am
My Parents
My family members
My wonderful friends
My Church family
My Al Anon family
All of the people that may read this and get help

ACKNOWLEDGMENTS

To Self-Publishing School and all of my author friends (too many to mention - I don't want to leave any one out.)

My accountability buddy, Kelly Walk Hines

Kimberly Gordon, my cover designer, editor, and formatter. Thank you for your brilliance and inspiration.

Christopher Moss, thank you for your help and encouragement.

Jacqui Trammel, technical assistance

The Shift Happens Launch Tribe

INTRODUCTION

Do you wonder what your true purpose or destiny is? Would you actually love to hear the Father's voice speaking to you?

Do you feel like the call of your life is different, maybe even misunderstood at times?

Do you feel like people's expectations put you in a box? The lack of variety and the lack of creativity can start pulling you underground. Pretty soon you're stuck in the mold of status quo. Everyone starts looking the same, sounding the same, and doing the same things.

This happened to me. I kept getting quieted and held underground. That's probably a pretty normal thing, but I met with the right folks that started digging me out. Little by little my voice started breaking through. I pushed up through the soil to find the sun and rain and the right nourishment that I needed to grow. Every flower that the Father made blooms differently and the same is true with human beings. We are all different. We all have different gifts and it's time for these gifts to be discovered and sought out.

We want to help you hear the Father's voice and see that you

INTRODUCTION

are not a mistake and you have a special purpose! We want to help you bloom! We've been Restored to Bloom and we are coming to dig you out! We see little green sprouts beginning to break through the soil! It's time.

It's harvest time!

1

FROM A SEEDLING

Let me share a little about my life with you first. I was born in the mid1950's, which were pretty good times in America. I grew up in a peaceful home in a quiet subdivision with my mom, dad, brother, and dog. My dad was raised on a farm but wanted his own business to support his family. He made a good living at the auto body shop as he pursued the American dream. We went to church every Sunday morning and took family vacations every year. I have great memories and old home movies which my dad turned into videos for us. I was blessed with good roots.

There were times of boating, water skiing, and camping. We knew wonderful people. I was a teenager in the Seventies so I had "Cher Hair" down to my waist, but it was blonde. I was trying to find out who I was in this big old world! Which group did I fit in with? I seemed to fit in with everyone from the freaks to the jocks, to the nerds, and even the jerks, too.

I remember that many boys liked me, but if they were real nice and a little nerdy, I felt uncomfortable with them. I wanted to be with someone that was more of an underdog. I don't know if that made me feel important or if I thought I would be safe with them and they would never leave me? Maybe it made me feel in control of the situation, which I definitely was not. As an empath, I could feel deeply what was going on in their shoes and wanted to help them walk out of their hard place. What I had to learn was that not everyone is willing and ready to do that. I spent a big part of my life learning this lesson.

Being a teenager in the 70's led to many challenges. I latched onto my boyfriend at age fifteen. This was the beginning of my identity for many, many years.

The first trauma occurred when we were sitting at my boyfriend's parent's house at an Easter dinner and he took a spin on a three wheel motorcycle. About a half hour later he ran into the house covered in blood with his mouth and eye torn open. We rushed him to the hospital. His face was swollen, his eye had to be rebuilt with new bones, and his mouth had to be repaired. The back wheel of his motorcycle had caught on a concrete barrel and flipped him over. A couple months later we went to the prom. He was still beat up.

I wasn't ready to get married after graduation, like many of my friends did. I had a family backing me up to do whatever career I chose, which was more than some people that I knew had. My dad suggested I take some business courses at the junior college. I tried that and it just wasn't me. I told him that I wanted to go to beauty school and become a hairstylist. He agreed to pay for it, but only if I stuck with it. So he paid a whopping nine hundred dollars for me to go to beauty school in the Seventies. And I did stick with it and I am still doing it to this day, forty-four years later.

While I was going to beauty school, we did lots of roller sets and I wondered how I was going to stand doing that every week. I was thrilled when I got out of school and a big salon opened in our area with blow dry cuts, perms, and highlights. That was my cup of tea. My personality likes variety. The people that I have had sitting in my chair all of these years are a gift from my dad and also my Heavenly Father. Sometimes I was listening to what was happening in my client's life and sometimes they were listening to what I was going through. These were divine moments.

Another trauma happened when I was in beauty school. I got a call at the school one day saying a poisonous snake had bitten my boyfriend and they weren't sure he would make it. I rushed to the hospital. My mom and her friends were praying. The hospital staff ordered an anti-venom and had it flown in from Texas, and he survived.

These things started to change my perspective. Several more traumas happened over the next several years, which I have documented in my first book, *Shift Happens: Turning Your Stumbling Blocks into Stepping Stones.*

You know what? I am thankful that I had faith to believe I was going to make it and somehow crawl out of the whole hot mess. That was also a gift from my Heavenly Father. I am grateful that I lived to tell about it. I'm thankful for the people that never stopped believing in me. I'm thankful for the ability to help others now. I'm thankful that my Father put Marty and I together and that we are helping people sort out their lives together.

If you have had similar things happening to you over and over, you can get to the root of it and stop thinking that you are a bad person who will never get it together. There are reasons that things happen in a person's life.

Empathy and codependency were two of my biggest reasons. Codependency is a form of addiction to helping and fixing people. It goes right along with being an empathetic person. Those who do not understand codependency may think they are being honorable by helping others live their lives.

I've worked hard to overcome this in my own life and now my big heart doesn't get me into so much trouble. I can use it in a more constructive way. Codependency is hard to detect because many times there are scriptures that seem to encourage it:

> *Peter asked Jesus, "How many times should I forgive my brother or sister who sins against me? Up to seven times?"Jesus answered, "I tell you, not seven times, but seventy times." (Matthew 18:21 NIV)*

We have to be sure that we do not take things that are said out of context. That doesn't mean to forgive someone who is beating you, cheating on you, or destroying your life in some way. When life starts going downhill, that's usually a sign to me that things are out of balance. In those cases, forgiving and loving is better done from a distance than up close.

I had to learn how to have boundaries and how to set them. Someone could be literally distracting your life from the way it is supposed to be. We have to be in charge of our own lives and what comes in and goes out. I am grateful that I have discernment now and can sense what direction something is going to go. We all need to pray for the gift of discernment and surround ourselves with reliable people who can point out our blind spots.

Stay open to learning, so that you can keep your roots from becoming mushy and rotten. It may take me some time to get something, but eventually it will stick. I try to listen to what someone is saying to me and I ponder it out with what my Father is saying to my heart. I want my will to be His will. He knows best. This is like healthy soil coming to me with lovely fresh sunshine and rainwater; a new starting place.

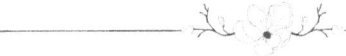

I started out so bright and shining,
Through many days so blissful and free.
Then trauma set in and dampened the bloom,
Many times too foggy to see.
~Jill Rogers~

2

AS I UNDERSTOOD

Life sometimes throws you so many lemons and curveballs that you need time to regroup. Being raised in a dysfunctional home full of addictions and escapism brings plenty of challenges. Children are taught to deny their feelings or at least not share them.

For example: A six year old boy comes up to his mother and says, "There's something about that guy that creeps me out!" The mom then answers, "No, there is nothing wrong with that guy." The discussion is over and closed.

Or a child asks their Father, "Dad, why do you drink so much? My friend's dads don't drink like you do." The Dad answers, "Don't you ever ask that again." Discussion closed.

Or someone comes down with cancer and has had much prayer surrounding them but is getting worse and worse. Instead of having empathy for the sick person, those praying tell him (or her) "You would get well if you had more faith. You are not doing something right or it would be gone." Discussion closed.

Any comment that isn't loving or nurturing is not coming from our Heavenly Father. They come from hurting, wounded,

SHIFT HAPPENS: RESTORED TO BLOOM

bruised people that probably need their hearts softened and healed inside.

When I chose many years ago to walk through the doors of Al-Anon Family Groups, which is for families that are dealing with alcoholism, I embarked on a journey that began to put the pieces of the puzzle of faith and life together for me.

Step number 3 of the 12 Steps is:

---

*"3. We made a decision to turn our will and our lives over to the care of God **as we understood Him**."*

If you present this to the three people above that I mentioned, how do you think they understand God?

They might picture The Father as someone that is cold, not very empathetic, understanding or even in their reality. They might see a God that gives them no voice. Wouldn't you?

Well...*the God of my understanding* is not just randomly throwing me scriptures that don't make sense to me. He is my Heavenly Father; He is clearly speaking to me what I need for each day. The relationship I have with Him is so loving that I know He will never run out on me, belittle me, or think I shouldn't have said something! He wants us to pour out all of our feelings to Him so He can help us sort things out. He is clearly telling me what I need each day, and can do the same for you.

He loves me so clearly and knows that I don't need a harsh, condescending voice speaking to me to get my attention. That is like rain beating against me so hard that it can knock me down. I listen to His voice because I know it is wise counsel to help my life and make me grow.

I love the scriptures and what they say and how they minister to me. I remember a time when the *"as I understood Him"* meant staying away from *anything* that made me feel like I was in trouble. I needed to build trust with God and receive His goodness, and grow.

"But they will never follow a stranger; in fact, they will run away from him because they do not recognize a stranger's voice." (*John 10:5 NIV*)

This verse is talking about sheep following their master and I have literally had to stay away from the wrong voice that is not God *as I understand Him.* If the voice does not give me growth, clarity, direction, or solutions, then I don't need that voice. If the voice is giving me lies and not truth, it is the wrong voice. The right voice restores me over and over again. It waters me and refreshes me and gives me just the right nutrients, and can do the same for you.

As we go on through this book you will see that there are different things along the path that helped me with faith, and can help you too. Restoring the Foundations has been a great resource for us to receive and learn how to minister a deeper level of healing. You will see how miraculously we kept being pulled onto the path over and over, until we received and attained everything we needed.

My life has been full of many paths, valleys, and mountains. I've learned from it all that nothing has been wasted! I am overjoyed to take everything that I have learned to help others understand their journey and find their true identity, purpose, and destiny!

I hope this will help you get in touch with God *as you understand Him.* It's not about religious rules. It's about a relationship with a God that can walk with you every day, help you get your life together, and avoid the voice telling you to go the wrong way!

If you have read my book *Shift Happens,* you have seen that my life has been a series of calamities but one of education for helping others through calamities and trauma. I can see now, after many of the things that I have learned, that being able to feel God with my heart was a gift and it really did help me survive, bringing miracles into my life. It helped me take risks that I needed to take and brought heaven to earth for me in many situations.

Just having faith in your head is not enough; it has to be in your heart. That is the kind of relationship with the Father that we hope you have, and we want to help if you haven't been able to attain it. It is for everyone, no one on this planet is rejected!

3

SEEDTIME AND HARVEST

"As long as the earth endures, seedtime and harvest, cold and heat, summer and winter, day and night will never cease." (Genesis 8:22, NIV)

The circle of life centers around seedtime and harvest. A seed from a male is placed into a female and by some miracle that we can't even imagine, they connect and a human being is formed.

With a plant or flower, the male plants produce pollen which is then carried to the female plant by birds, bees, insects, or wind. The pollen makes its way inside the female plant, where it connects with the ovaries and produces seeds. The female plants then project the seeds outward to be dropped in the surrounding soil to be multiplied.

Seeds come in many forms, shapes, and sizes. They all come with an outer shell, called the seed coat, and an inside called the embryo with an endosperm which feeds the plant. The seed coat protects the plant; it has special chemicals in it that know the right time for the plant to start growing. Different seeds grow at different paces. When seeds are not in dirt, they are dormant and can stay like that for a long, long time.

To grow, they need the right temperature, water, and the right amount of light. When the embryo is planted in the right amount of moist soil, they get the signal to start growing. The seed coat will then let just a little water into the embryo. The endosperm is there with just the right amount of food and energy. It's like the embryo's own backpack of snacks. As it gets enough water the embryo kicks out a "foot," not like our foot, but the beginning of the roots.

Yes, the first thing that a seed grows is roots. They push down deeper and deeper to keep the plant from turning over, and finding more minerals to nourish the plant.

Once the roots are established, the seed pops out a shoot. It fights through the dirt until it gets to the sun and then we can say that it "sprouted." Now the plant doesn't need the endosperm anymore because the sun and water are providing the nourishment that it needs. The leaves, then sprout to bring the shade and protection that it needs to stay alive.

The rich soil, the sun, and the water represent the nutrients that our Father brings to us. Prayer, learning the words of life in the Scriptures and having people full of faith all around us can pull us up, up, up to the place that we need to be. The place where we can stand strong, have our voice, and say what we need to say to help others come up to the place where they need to be.

The water from the rain came
The dirt plowed just right
I stood up taller and taller
I knew it wasn't by my might.
~Jill Rogers~

4

SEEDS SOWN THIS YEAR

I started off the year by bringing a group of ladies into my house to make vision boards for the upcoming year. Putting down the things that are inside of us is a powerful way to invite them into our lives, drawing those things to us.

As you look at the vision that you've created it becomes real in your brain, heart, and body. You begin to experience this future event in the present. You actually start living it out.

"He took him outside and said, "Look up at the sky and count the stars—if indeed you can count them." Then He said to him, "So shall your offspring be." (Genesis 15:5)

A lady that was present that day told me that bringing everyone together would draw these things to myself ten times over. Wow! I could hardly imagine that happening when she said it, but I have received many blessings this year and I do know that when you plant a seed, there is a harvest time. We planted many seeds and many things have come forth. We've been blessed with enough finances to pay off our debt, met many new connections, and had the opportunity to dig many people out of their "stuck" place. We have also experienced more of the Father's rest.

THE 12 STEPS OF RECOVERY

The 12 Steps of Recovery was the first process that helped me find my identity and what was tripping me up in my life. It taught me how to dig deep and get ahold of some reality. I would suggest this for anyone that needs a beginning to break out of dysfunctional patterns in life. I still go to a recovery meeting every week and I love having a safe place to be accountable to someone. These steps have been blessed seeds sown into my life.

I personally love the 12 Steps of Recovery, but I don't look at anything that I mention as the only cure-all. I look at them as my seeds to recovery and freedom in my life. I personally want more than anything for people to find a loving, nurturing Heavenly Father that can help them find their own pathway to freedom. These steps are the roots in my life for many of the things that I do.

There are many places of recovery that offer these steps, such as meetings for addictions, for families of addicts, and children of addicts. These meetings offer a wealth of information and healing from dealing with all forms of addictions. Some churches offer Celebrate Recovery. This is a Christian recovery program that was designed and built around the 12 Steps of Alcoholics Anonymous.

Each of the 12 Steps leads to the next one. They take us through a time of addressing things from our past and getting rid of them so we can be free. It is a good place to be accountable and learn how to walk out a more functional life; a place where we can build trust. The meetings have been a great place for me to build trust with a nonjudgmental atmosphere.

1. We admitted that we are powerless over whatever we are dealing with in our life—that our lives have become unmanageable. (In other words, you haven't been able to conquer it on your own.) Are you able to see something in your life that you haven't been able to conquer? Maybe even something that can lead to making your life unmanageable?
2. We came to believe that a Power greater than ourselves could restore us to sanity. (This is such a gracious way to take a hurting, wounded, and beat up person and slowly lead them to The Father, if they decide to make that choice.) Can you do this? I know it may be hard if you have been treated badly.
3. We made a decision to turn our will and our lives over to the care of God *as we understood Him.* (This removes any hurtful ways that The Father has been presented to us. Hurting people need the grace to start with little loving baby steps.)
4. We made a searching and fearless moral inventory of ourselves. (This includes good and bad things about ourselves, leading us to truth and reality about ourselves.) Can you list ten good things about you?

Now list ten things that you do not like, are sorry for, or want to change about you.

5. We admitted to God, to ourselves, and to another human being the exact nature of our wrongs. (This is a safe way to open up past things and bring them to the light in order to heal from them.) If you have a person that you can trust, it would be great to have them help you do this one. Admitting our faults is a great way to humble ourselves.
6. We were entirely ready to have God remove all these defects of character. (Letting all these hurtful things go to your loving Father, who is not mad at you. He loves you and wants you to be free.) Are you ready to be free from the things that torment you?
7. We humbly asked Him to remove our shortcomings. (We admit that we can't do it alone and ask Him to do it.) Can you let these things go to God *as you understand Him?*
8. We made a list of all persons we had harmed and became willing to make amends to them all. (We let go of our "flaws" little by little, such as things that have been tormenting us.) Can you think of people that you may have hurt? Even unintentionally?
9. We made direct amends to such people wherever possible, except when to do so would injure them or others. (This brings more humility and unloading the baggage that we've carried around.) Do you need to apologize to anyone, or come clean about anything? Only if it would not injure them or others.
10. We continued to take personal inventory and when we were wrong promptly admitted it. (Freedom is an ongoing process.) In our daily quiet time, which we all need by the way, we need to come clean every day.
11. We sought through prayer and meditation to improve

SHIFT HAPPENS: RESTORED TO BLOOM

our conscious contact with God *as we understood Him,* praying only for knowledge of His will for us and the power to carry that out. (These things help keep that loving relationship with the Father)
12. After having had a spiritual awakening as a result of these steps, we tried to carry this message to others, and to practice these principles in all our affairs. (We received freedom and are paying it forward to others.) Paying it forward helps *us* stay free!

WE ARE available to help in any way to help you through this process. I will provide our contact info for anyone that may need it. There are places where we get more in depth with these steps and dig deeper when the person is ready. We will list references, too. I have personally learned that The Father can show up and help in many ways. He can even show up in life circumstances, a movie, a walk that we may take, a song that you haven't heard for decades, and so many other ways.

It doesn't all take place behind stained glass inside the four walls. I have seen so many miracles take place in these rooms with people that don't even know if they are worthy of it. The truth is that we are **all** worthy of it! Never forget that. We are **all** worthy of it. That's pretty awesome news isn't it? The Father is **NEVER** mad at us. He's not mad...period. He's full of love!

We can move as slowly as we need to on these steps. We can go at our own pace and when we are ready for it. It is not a race, it is a process. We don't just arrive at a place of perfection, we have to keep working it out and walking it out.

The recovery program helped me to release my addiction to religion and self-righteousness. As I walked through this process, I realized that some of my issues had been passed down through the generations. I also realized that some of the decisions I've made and some of the traumatic life experiences I've had have messed up my normal growth process in life.

So, the first thing that I broke free from in this program was self-righteousness. There are many personalities that can get wrapped up in religion and become egotistical, dogmatic, and judgmental to name a few, due to lack of humility and not tapping into the true spirit of what God is all about. Life is not just about rules.

I love the way recovery helps us deal with our flaws in a safe, nonjudgmental way. I learned at the recovery meetings that I need to let go of things and not carry them, that my Father has stepped in and done many things for me through grace. This has taught me how to let go of performance-based thinking, security blankets, and the need to fix everything myself. This program and these steps can do the same for you. I encourage you to go through them for life-changing results.

"The first three steps taught me to give up. Four, Five and Six taught me how to own up. Seven, Eight and Nine taught me how to make up. Ten, Eleven and Twelve taught me how to grow up."
~#SOBERVETS

6

DIGGING OUT THOSE ROOTS

Our adventure with Restoring the Foundations started in the summer of 2016. We were a part of a fellowship where it was being presented. We were really getting into it when we got a call inviting us to receive more training. The training would be a week long, three hours north of us. We were presented a home that would host us and a couple that became a divine connection for us to this day. This couple has sown many seeds into our lives.

We had such a positive experience staying there. We rode together to the meetings; we spoke into each other's lives and still do to this day. We ate together with others that were there, and it was such a good feeling to fit in.

The first part of our training was called "Issue Focused." We were ministered to by a team and then participated in team that ministered to others. This felt like heaven to me because I had been trained in so many different ways for this and it seemed to be my life passion, purpose, and destiny.

When I experienced my first session of being ministered to, I just cried and cried. They were good tears, tears of release. I had been a part of so many places where people were simply not being real. Because I had been a part of the recovery meetings and had seen people being so honest and open about what is going on with them, it was hard for me to stand the contrast.

My experiences at church were more about looking like you had it all together, instead of *"confessing our faults so that we may be healed." (James 5:16)* Perhaps it wasn't intentional, but there seemed to be a focus on certain people's abilities, which others competed to aspire to. It just wasn't what I was called to do. No judgment or criticism, I just have to listen to the right voice and go the right direction.

When I arrived at this training, I was amazed people were actually talking about things that they were going through and not trying to pretend like they had it all together.

I agree with people being positive and I agree in believing for impossible things. I even believe in spontaneous healing but some patterns take a while to be sure that they are actually healed. If someone is just *thinking* they are healed, it will always come back around again to be dealt with. Having a safe place to be honest and deal with these things is wonderful!

Needless to say, it was quite a pleasant surprise to have the experience of a group of Christian people that I could be very real with! There are many hurting people that don't have a safe place to be real and certainly don't need any discouragement from being that way! My heart goes out to them.

I have also learned that denial is a huge part of the addictive process. The person is not in tune with what is really going on in their life. We have to face things in our life head on...reality is real! Everyday life is real!

My tears were from feeling lonely in the call of my life and not knowing how to incorporate it in my life. I was trying to get encouragement from the wrong places. But God, *as I understood Him* came through in a powerful way!

After going through this first Issue Focused session, I felt validated and affirmed. I was no longer looking at things from an orphan spirit or victim mindset. I was looking at the fact that I am just unique and have to stay around the things that welcome who I am, which are like fresh rain and sunshine.

I can remember feeling intimidated being in the first session. I didn't know if I could trust or not. Trust is something that is earned. Over the course of that week there was lots of trust built with these people. Trust seems to be an important thing for me. I think trust and relationship are important to God too.

In the Issue Focused ministry we only deal with one main issue in the person's life. We hit the issue in four different ways called the "Integrated Approach" which builds upon itself to produce freedom.

The Issue Focused session takes about three hours. The person receiving ministry fills out a PQ (Personal Questionnaire) which is turned into the ministry team before the first session. The first thing we deal with is "Sins of the Father and Curses" which is information about ancestors and the effects that they have had on the receiver's life. In this session we are dealing with only one issue that the person is struggling with but hitting it from all four angles. Second, is "Ungodly Beliefs," which are lies about ourselves that we have picked up along the way.

The PQ requests information that helps us know the lies that we are dealing with. The third is "Soul Spirit Hurts," which are memories in a person's life that we ask the Holy Spirit to heal. This session is my favorite.

Amazing things can happen in this session and the person usually gets a revelation about a memory and an understanding along with healing of the memory. It is so exciting to see someone freed from something that has bothered them for a long time.

Lastly, "Demonic Oppression" deals with the roots of the issue. These are like weeds ground up through the other three steps and pulled out easily in the final step. All of the steps work together to bring deep and lasting freedom. The ministry is not loud and forceful; it is gentle and nurturing. We are Restoring the

Foundations ministers and we love to minister to people that need our help.

After bringing these things to the surface and dealing with them, we can learn to look at life in a whole different way. I am not professing it to be a one cure-all method. It has been something very structured that we have been led into for inner health and freedom.

There were several leaders that we connected with in a positive way. At the end of the week of training and ministry, we learned of a deeper form of ministry that RTF offers called "Thorough Format." It involved six weeks of training in Abilene, Texas.

We looked at each other and wanted to go so bad but thought, "No way." Marty even asked if there was a place to park campers there. What's funny is we didn't even have one.

Time went on and we heard from the administrator at Abilene that there was a camper hook up there and I said, "Great, we don't have a camper." Ha!

When it got closer to time for this to start, we were asked to fill in for someone who normally helped in the kitchen. We didn't waste much time saying yes, though we had no idea what we were getting into. We both jumped in by faith. It was surely a test for everyone.

I'm very grateful to this day for the opportunity that we had to help us move forward. God truly made a way for us where there was none. While we didn't have the finances at the time, we were still available to sow some seeds into something very special. We certainly received much fresh rain and sunshine in return.

"Some people have only heard lies about themselves and we need to help them know the truth about who they really are. We can even speak what they truly are, into existence."
~Jill Rogers~

7

SWEET ABILENE

The site was an old World War II army training base. We pulled up and looked around.

The place was out in the desert with lots of sand and dust, but we came to love it there.

Marty and I had a cabin all to ourselves with two twin beds pushed together, a kitchen sink, a table, a shower, and a toilet. We had no wi-fi in the cabin and no TV, but I could get my Verizon signal there. Yay!

We washed our clothes and hung them out on the line to dry. The winds dried them fast.

We ate in a big building that looked like an army mess hall. In the six weeks we were there, I was the closest I have ever come to boot camp. It was a life-changing experience for both of us. There were leaders from all over the United States as well as missionaries from other countries.

It felt great to get away, almost like being in another country. The most exciting part was driving up a big steep mountain and reaching the huge cross up on top. The scenery was wonderful.

There were beautiful worship meetings, and prayer, and God's presence was amazing.

I wanted to jump ship several times while we were there, but we kept persevering through. We got to see first-hand the character and heart of these people that were probably used to gourmet meals and choices we were not presenting. We did our best and I think the people there had a love and compassion for what we were doing.

Finally, toward the end, the people noticed that we were struggling a bit and we had a meeting with the administrator of the whole event. She apologized for not being a hundred percent clear on some things. We just had to jump in and sink or swim. I remember when she looked at us and said, "I couldn't have done it without you." It made us realize that God was carrying the whole thing. We didn't say that we would do things perfectly; we just said that we would do it. In some situations that's all that matters, just showing up and doing it.

The way the whole thing was handled was quite amazing to me, and I needed to see that. I think when you are in a situation like that, you find out what is truly important. Sure, there would have been others more gifted at doing the meals, but God used the whole thing as an opportunity to work on all of us. I'm thankful that I didn't jump ship, but I'm sorry that the meals weren't excellent. We can surely learn from every experience!

After more people came, we had more help in the kitchen. We moved on to being ministered to and ministering to others. By having us serve others first, I think God was tilling the soil, preparing us in order to plant new seeds that would bloom and grow. This is when we stepped into new unchartered territories of learning and growing.

First, we ministered to someone with our trainers helping us. Being the type of person that has a hard time learning with someone watching me, I struggled through this part. Being brave and doing it afraid brought me into new things. I learned by being honest that problems would get resolved with this group of people. I was thankful that I could be my own genuine authentic self with whatever flaws come with it.

I do know for a fact that we do not need to pretend anything. Being honest about things is a valuable asset in this ministry and in any ministry helping others. I absolutely love the fact that these people were really out to help us get someplace, and not just throw us out.

The paperwork for what we were doing was new and felt quite intense sometimes. We even joked with our trainer and she would say that the paper vortex had struck again.

One morning, another trainer told our trainers that she felt Marty and I had both had pretty shattered lives and that when working with us, they needed to remember what was coming from our hearts was more important than how well we were doing paperwork. I was thankful to God for that! That gave us some peace and even our trainers more peace and understanding. This was another divine encounter.

Have you had encounters that seemed to be divine? Think right now about the way God has also taken care of you

During this phase I only had one time that I thought I couldn't go on. I got real and told them, we worked through it, and moved on with the rest of the ministry.

Finally, we reached the part where we were ministered to. I loved it. There were times of honesty and tears but it was worth it all.

I would go in the afternoons and Marty would go in the morning. We would have to come home, do some homework they assigned us, and go back the following day for the next part of ministry.

We did this for a week, which ended with us getting to go on a date night. We were finished cooking and ministering and were almost ready to head back home. We had a wonderful meal that night and a night of graduation. After six weeks in Texas, we had accomplished what we were sent there to do, and were forever changed.

Are you ready to be forever changed? We are trained in the Restoring the Foundations Ministry and would be happy to help you go through this process. I have learned that whatever is refreshing and brings nourishment to my life is like water and sunshine to my soul. I can't grow and come up higher and reach taller without these things. I also need to sow seeds into other's lives so that they may also grow.

8

BACK TO FAMILIAR SOIL

How do you return home to a new normal? How do you stay in the same surroundings and get along with the same people when you feel different and don't want to go back to the way you used to be? A turning point came when others started reaching out for help. They heard we had something to offer. I believe God knew this would help us keep moving forward, by helping them. So He kept sending them to us.

When we heard about the possibility of being a part of Restoring the Foundation's Healing House Network, I thought, "That sounds just like my destiny!"

I knew I wanted to help people receive the freedom that I had, but I felt a little conflicted. I had received my voice back during the RTF sessions so I wanted to help people in that way, yet I also thought that writing and telling my story could reach many more people.

I started writing my first book. I hadn't come far enough through the journey with RTF. I wrote more about the things that had happened up to that point, but then I gained the power to finish it. The fresh rain and sunshine were causing me to push up through the dirt and start to shine in my identity and destiny.

I plowed in and made a file cabinet just like the one that we were shown in Texas. I had even taken pictures of how to set it up. I couldn't stop doing it until I was finished, even though I really didn't think anyone would want what we had to offer.

People started coming to us, one by one, two by two. We honestly didn't know if anyone would want to go through the Thorough Format Ministry. The training was quite a commitment and investment. There are big ministries that will not let anyone be on staff that has not been through RTF Thorough Format Ministry.

James 5:16 (NIV) *"Therefore confess your sins to each other and pray for each other so that you may be healed.* (James 5:16 NIV)

When we walk someone through this, we feel freer ourselves. We develop a bond with these people that you can't imagine. Some of them have probably never had someone sit down with them and listen to them for so many hours in all of their lives.

We love helping people break down lies about themselves. We love helping them find their true selves and what they are called to do. We love helping them connect to the Father's voice. We were very grateful for the ones that reached out to us and entrusted their lives to us so we could help in any way that we could.

There were some that had been hurt and rejected by so many people that they believed they were worthless. There were others that had been handed over to so much darkness, even by their parents. It's hard to reprogram oneself after that kind of trauma. They were trapped in a victim mindset and needed to be overcomers instead.

The whole time we were ministering to these different people, I was writing my book. Finding the time to do healing sessions and finish it was challenging. The power to do this did not come from me. It came from a power greater than me, and it was meant to be heard.

Thorough Format Ministry covers the same four things as Issue Focused but is more intense and is more than one issue. The receiver fills out a form called "My Story" which is several pages with thorough questions about your life. It can be a ministry to an individual or a couple. The couple's ministry can include renewing their marriage covenant at the end and taking communion together.

The sessions begin with an interview so the ministry team can understand how to best minister to the receiver. The ministry covers the same four areas as the Issue Focused but is more thorough. The sessions end up being around fifteen hours of ministry.

During the "Spirit Soul Hurts" session of Thorough Format Ministry is when I received healing of a memory when I was raped at the age of twenty-three. The rapist had threatened to kill me if I told anyone. Because of fear, I believe, someone close to me asked, "You aren't going to tell anyone are you?" Both of these things working together took away my voice, not in a literal way but in a more subconscious way that showed up later. It didn't keep me from talking about the incident and getting him arrested and off the street; but it did affect my voice and my destiny.

Can you see how the enemy can work to steal and rob your destiny? The sessions I went through helped me unlock my purpose and destiny. I am so grateful for that, because I knew that it was in there, I was just stifled. Now I am free to be me. Have you experienced any trauma that has left you not being your true self? Or maybe you're not sure who your true self is.

All of the different traumas that Marty and I have been through have been incredible training for helping others. People feel like we are someone that can understand, because we have been there too.

This whole journey has been a process. After I published my

book, I started seeing lots of possibilities and directions to go. One night I dreamed of a fork in the road. The path I had been traveling on was going off in a different direction. So within a few weeks we started filling out the paperwork to be part of the Healing House Network. We even went as far as having a person come to qualify us for the RTF Healing House only to realize that God was calling us to help in our region and the people in our local church. He was also calling me to finish this book.

The day after we made the decision to remain in our region, my Father planted some finances in our hands and confirmed that we had made the right choice. We realized that the things we had learned were stepping stones, not landing places.

We have studied and learned many different freedom paths and wanted to offer them to those that we come in contact with. We wanted to meet all the different needs from Recovery to Restoration. Millennials love simplicity and we have tried to be sensitive to that as well.

We are learning and tapping into ways to keep sowing more seeds into others. We know that when we are blessed with things that water and nourish us, we have to pass them on to others. That keeps the cycle of life going.

"She silently stepped out of the race that she never wanted to be in, found her own lane, and proceeded to win."
-Anonymous

9

TOP TEN SONGS

*A*n author friend of mine, Christopher Moss, has written seven books in the last two years. In his last book entitled *Fearless Author Mindset Workbook*, he mentioned that he has a top ten list of songs that keeps him inspired. It was so funny that one of the songs he mentioned just happened to come on the radio when Marty and I took off in our new boat. It was "Baker Street" by Gerry Rafferty. When I heard this song and the wind started blowing through my hair I started crying!

The song, along with the feeling of riding in the boat, triggered many memories and brought much healing to me. I was brought up water skiing and almost every home movie that my dad made when I was growing up had us boating as a family and my brother and I water skiing. My Father showed up and it was like fresh water, giving me trickles of nourishment and inspiration to be me, the "me" that I am created to be with a past, a present, and a future; the person that was created with a voice to help restore others in the same way.

I'm going to ask you to make a top ten list of songs for you. A few of mine are:

- "Baker Street" by Gerry Rafferty
- "King" by Lauren Aquilina
- "Fear is a Liar" by Zach Williams
- "King of My Heart" by Steffany Gretzinger

I felt so much from heaven when I took my friend Christopher's idea and listed all of my songs. As I started listening to them I felt so much freedom, as if I was in my own mini-retreat. What a powerful tool.

The song "Baker Street" made me feel a divine connection with my Father. I looked up when this song was released and it was in 1978, five years after I graduated from high school. I had been through a couple of small traumas but it was before my first marriage and before I was raped. It took me back to a time when I was more me. Thank God I am now restored and it feels so good. I'm probably better off than I was before I went through all of the traumas.

The song "King" by Lauren Aquilina is a positive, beautiful song that my granddaughter got brave and sang one night at an open mic night in her little town. It was something none of us were expecting and I was so excited to see how spontaneous she was in doing this. It expressed her heart as she sang those words, the way that she likes to help people. She did a great job and I'm so happy that she had the opportunity to do it.

The song "Fear is a Liar" by Zach Williams, is a song that my son-in-law, Justin, sang at church on Mother's Day and I was excited to be there. What an amazing blessing it was. Justin has walked through some difficulties in life and it was a miracle for him to sing that song. I'm grateful that he is Beth's husband and dad to her three girls. I've learned so much from him and Beth as a couple, and they are handling their family so well.

The song, "King of My Heart" by Steffany Gretzinger is a song that speaks to my soul. My daughter Lindsay's wife, Rachel, sent it to me. It was golden nuggets coming to me from heaven. I'm grateful for Rachel and Lindsay in our lives, and the things that I have learned from them both.

These songs represented lots of memories and emotions. Some of the older songs I had stopped listening to because they weren't serving me well in that particular season, but with healing and time, my roots have grown deeper and stronger now, with more strength to hang onto my identity.

I encourage you to find songs that mean something to you and inspire you. Start a top ten list if you haven't, I'm sure that you will find music, of all kinds, very therapeutic.

"I can't explain the way I feel but I can find a song that can."
-Unknown

10

COMMUNION WITH GOD MINISTRIES

We have been taking people through prayer sessions and I have been designing courses on a support group page on Facebook. I am very grateful for the model that Communion with God Ministries offers. It was something that came right when I needed it. I sent them an email asking if they had heard of Restoring the Foundations Ministries and they said that they had a wonderful relationship with them, which made me more comfortable with this ministry.

Their book and course are called Unleashing Healing Power Through Spirit-Born Emotions

Mark and Patty Virkler bring another piece to the puzzle of designing courses and providing people with freedom. Through these healing prayers I have even started designing meditations that people can listen to after we take them through sessions, to help them keep their healing fresh and alive.

Mark Virkler writes: "I have come to the conclusion that faith, when coupled with the Kingdom emotions of compassion and gratitude, brings forth miracles. When used together, the synergy of these elements releases sufficient spiritual power to overcome the hard-wired circuits in my mind and body and produce a life-transforming miracle."

I have met many people who have trained themselves to ignore feelings. I personally could not have survived all the traumas in my life if I had never faced my feelings and experienced healing from them. I needed my memories healed. This course is brilliant to me and what Father has shown me.

Mr. Virkler even writes that he used to "scorn" emotions and think that they were part of the "soulish realm," which is what I almost did at one time. I sure can't say that was freedom, it was more like control. I would say it's something that has to be balanced out. Too much control can bring about a lack of joy, peace, compassion and gratitude. If we try to chase away the bad feelings, some good feelings go with them. Numbness sets in and our life can get out of whack. We can actually lose power.

This course teaches that walking with God is as much of a heart thing as a mind thing. I sometimes have a hard time explaining my experiences. I need to feel it in my heart and have many vibrant experiences to keep my relationship with God alive and real. Many people would pride themselves on the scriptures that they knew so well and how to teach things so well, but I think it's so important to have the tangible real life experiences happening too. It helped to hear something straight from Father and experience something relevant shortly after. Then I knew He was speaking to me.

There has been so much emphasis placed on the mind and what people know about the scriptures, than the Rhema (a quickening that we hear or feel straight from God) or even the emotions behind things hasn't been emphasized as much. Actually hearing my Father's voice has healed me from the effects of trauma and survive.

Surrendering our will and our lives to Father is what helps us overcome.

We have to feel safe and be able to trust before we can do that.

We need to take our eyes off of imperfect people that are misrepresenting God as we understand Him and we need to forgive them. I have enjoyed the activations in this course that are leading me to hear the things that I needed to hear straight from the Father's heart to my heart.

Father is good, kind, loving, and on our side if we turn our will over to Him and trust Him. Go at your own pace. God has told me during these meditation and prayer times;

"Very truly I tell you, whoever believes in me will be doing the works that I have been doing and they will do even greater things than these, because I am going to the Father." (John 14:12 NIV)

The actual thing that I heard was, "You will do greater things than I have done." When I actually heard it from my Father, it gave me permission to do it. I think that it could mean because of all of the media and different things available, we will be able to do greater things than Him. I also keep hearing from God that He is the one giving me these ideas so don't hold back. Okay, I will keep them coming. We all need to be hearing these things straight from the Father.

I emailed Mark Virkler and shared with him what a miracle it was for me to get to be listening to his audio recordings and that I had actually been making some of my own to share with people. I told him that I would refer them to his website and asked if he minded if I used some of his words in my audios. He gave me permission to use his words and that has blessed me so much.

I have been doing the meditations from this course every day and have been restored so much from the time of desperation when Father was so close to me that I couldn't do anything without Him. I have been hearing His voice about what He wants me to create in my writing and present to others. He is speaking through me. The meditations are changing me and I am enjoying creating my own, along with sharing and connecting people with forms of transformation, vision boards, and journaling. This whole process is helping me sleep better, too.

I am not the only one that feels this way about how Christianity has been represented. The enemy of our soul has been working a long time to distort, twist, and make God appear to be the bad guy instead of the good guy. Lies! I am grateful that Father Himself has never appeared to be anything but positive to me. I never felt like He was mad at me. Even through all of my mess-ups and poor decisions, I knew He loved me. I know He was probably frustrated with what I was doing at times, but He never turned his back on me.

I have seen that after all of the traumas that happened in my life so close to each other, it was truly a miracle that I haven't had some kind of serious illness or even depression attach itself to me. I believe it's because I was constantly reaching out for help, working through the trauma, and dealing with all of the feelings I was having. I was an open book, surrounded by the support and love of many people.

These books and courses are available for anyone that is interested in learning more. There is a wealth of information available.

MEDITATIONS: FRESH WATER AND RAIN

I have now begun designing my own meditations from the examples I've seen from Dr. Mark Virkler's course. I'm gradually putting them on my YouTube channel, which is Pier 7 Healing House. This has been such a joy for me. Listeners have encouraged me to keep making more.

These meditations are actually communing with the Father and hearing His answers from heaven. I'm hoping to help people be transformed, healed, and restored by listening to them. Hearing clear direction from the Father is such a blessing.

"Change your heart; Change your life. Spiritual meditation makes this possible. You close your eyes and see the scene once again of God's promises toward you concerning your life, your health, your family, your future, and your destiny. As you gaze upon this you are transformed.

"For our light and momentary troubles are achieving for us an eternal glory that far outweighs them all. So we fix our eyes not on what is seen, but on what is unseen, since what is seen is temporary, but what is unseen is eternal.(2 Corinthians 4:17 & 18 NIV)"

> *"As you rehearse this destiny or promise, it becomes familiar to you. Your heart and mind are rewired to believe and receive and respond in faith and obedience to that which you are gazing upon. Your body changes! Thousands of genes are turned on or off to make this future your possibility today. Gaze upon this new reality, observing every detail, memorizing them, rewiring your mind and heart to receive."*
>
> *"Combine the emotions of compassion, joy, thankfulness, and excitement knowing what you are seeing on the screen inside your mind is your true reality in Christ! Kingdom emotion bathes your body in neurochemistry that would be present if that future event were actually happening now. You are experiencing a taste of this future experience now!"*
>
> ~Dr. Mark Virkler

I could not have explained that better myself. Meditation and visualization can actually shift your physical body. I have experienced it and I encourage you to experience it if you have not. I am not just talking about naming it and claiming it, I am talking about actual transformation.

As we are going through this, ask God to give you a sign during that day to confirm that what you are hearing from Him is true. That's how alive the communication can become. I pray that everyone can have this kind of relationship with their Heavenly Father. To know that He hears you, loves you, and answers you. I encourage you to pursue this. You deserve it.

> *"Now the Lord is the Spirit, and where the Spirit of the Lord is, there is freedom. And we all, who with unveiled faces contemplate the Lord's glory, are being transformed into his image with ever-increasing glory, which comes from the Lord, who is the Spirit."* (2 Corinthians 3:17-18 NIV)

JILL ROGERS

You need to know something? Ask God He will show you the answer!
~Marty Rogers~

12

MY CHEERLEADER OF DREAMS

Terri Savelle Foy is a cheerleader of dreams. Marty and I have listened to her many mornings and she is so good about inspiring and encouraging me. For the last two years, I've hosted a gathering of ladies here at the beginning of the year to design vision boards for ourselves. Terri's book "Dream It, Pin It, Live It" has great stories and her pointers were so inspiring. She shares so many success stories about herself and others. I have always loved success stories.

The word I picked for 2019 was "brave." When I started the year, I had no intention of writing another book, but the promptings started coming to me. Many things crossed my path that set this book in motion. I put "Action with Books (wisdom)" on my vision board and it was called out into the atmosphere, so why wouldn't it start happening? I am receiving more and more wisdom to share with others.

I placed many items on my vision board in faith and had no idea they would actually happen. Even small details like my decor have been fulfilled. We remodeled our kitchen, we bought new living room furniture, and revamped our dining room furniture to match the new kitchen decor better. I wasn't even planning on doing all of that when I wrote it down and didn't really think that it would happen.

There is nothing that I would rather do than help others transform their lives. I believe it is one of the reasons I was put on this earth.

"Accept the things we can't change, and the thing that we can change is usually us."
~Jill Rogers

13

STARTING THE DAY OFF RIGHT

Can your morning routines really change your life? I think the answer is yes. Terri Savelle Foy shares the morning habits that successful people do. I like the way she brings God and scriptures into her teachings in a nonjudgmental way. It's inspiring to see that discipline and changing your routine can change your life and open doors.

She shares that our morning is the best time to set the tone for the rest of the day. I have seen this to be true. It can be the golden hour.

The three keys that lead you to your dreams:

- Twenty minutes of praying or meditating (I like to journal as well.)
- Twenty minutes of exercise
- Twenty minutes of reading

I started doing this at the beginning of this year. It brought more clarity in my life, as well as confidence and wisdom. It centered and grounded my life. If it seems hard for you to do, just try it for twenty-one days. Small goals are good.

If we can give our attention to these three things every morning, we can begin to "shift" our mindsets to more positive things. If we can journal and hear God's voice we can "shift" our hearts to believe new things. When we can start believing things, they can actually start happening. I have learned that getting our mind, our will, and our emotions all working together is the Kingdom combination for freedom and success in our lives.

I recently picked up Terri's book, "Declutter Your Way To Success." Terri shares that her first revelation along her path to success was to clean up and clean out. She jokes in the book about how she was expecting something more exciting, but that simple process put her on the road to success, opening many doors. It is a way of tilling the soil, sowing seeds of humility in her heart.

When I started reading this book, I didn't feel motivated to start doing it. Then I got a call from my uncle whom I hadn't seen in many years. He was coming and wanted to spend the night. We only have one bedroom on the main floor of our house and he has trouble seeing because he is getting ready to have eye surgery. That meant sleeping in my bed in my room. Don't get me wrong, the rest of my house is not too bad, we host a community group from our church here once a week, so many rooms are just fine. But my bedroom closet is a mess. Company coming can sure get you motivated to plow in and do something very quickly. It feels so good to have a clean, organized closet. I even color-coded my clothes on my side of the closet. My uncle and his wife came and said they slept wonderfully in my room that night.

I would encourage anyone that may be needing help with clutter or organization to read this book. Small changes in our lives can lead to big changes in our paths, tilling the soil for change.

"Sometimes you can't move forward out of old mindsets until you do something really scary that you can't do, to make it happen!"

~Jill Rogers

14

WEIGHT WATCHERS

Weight Watchers has also been something valuable in my life. I started it around twelve years ago after putting on some weight during menopause. It has helped me develop a lifestyle of eating better instead of dieting.

Once you get down to a goal weight, you can become a lifetime member and only have to weigh in once a month. If your weight is within your goal weight then you no longer have to pay anything for meetings. It's good for me to pop in monthly because I love the incentive and you get recipes and ideas.

I have found that if I stick to it fairly well and keep up with my exercises, that I'm good as far as staying in my proper weight range. I try to walk a mile around three or four times a week.

I love to be around people and I love to be accountable, it helps me to stay on track with what I'm doing. I mainly use it as a maintenance program. I can live a few months pretty relaxed with it and then the pounds start creeping back on, so I have to start plowing in and being a little more serious about it, which means keeping track of my points and tracking my food intake. Weight Watchers has helped so many people reach their goals. I like easy things that flow well with my life so I will keep doing it.

Have you been struggling with your weight? Or are you in denial about how much weight you've gained? There is hope for change. Anything we decide to change can change. Don't put it off any longer. If this isn't the right program for you, I encourage you to find what works and do it. It's never too late and it's not going to change without some action.

If something is holding you back and you can't start, please contact us. Sometimes past trauma can stop us from trusting and getting the help we need. I will be your biggest encouragement for taking that first step.

You can do it! You are valuable and you deserve to be healthy and to enjoy your life! No matter how much you have to lose!

15

2019: RESTORED TO BLOOM

This year started out with a real bang. I had the ladies over to do the vision boards and set some goals. We started remodeling our house in January, so keeping some of the goals I set was a little messy but I managed pretty well.

So many people that we knew passed away this year, including my coach Julie Languille. She helped me learn how to present deeper level healing to the world. Julie was a very brilliant woman of God and was so confident in building me up and loving me. She worked personally with me on calls. She could do amazing things with technology, and I was right there alongside watching her so I did pick some of it up.

Somehow I just knew that there was something going on and I knew before she passed away that we would not be finishing together. There were traumas in her life for the entire time we worked together. She started out living in Hawaii, but volcanic lava swept through her area, forcing her to evacuate. She handled everything with such grace and poise.

Julie began having headaches and was diagnosed with a malignant brain tumor. She passed away peacefully in her sleep. It was a learning experience just to see her walk through all of these things. Trauma has surrounded me through my whole adult life. I have experienced many losses through divorce and abandonment, but the losses this year have been through death.

Here are some of the things I've learned about life and death:

- Make life more intentional every day.
- Realize how fragile life is, and that if you don't do things now, they may not get finished.
- Care less about what people think and be braver to mention God more.
- Enjoy the people that will let me enjoy them and let go of the ones that don't.
- Don't sweat the small stuff, and most things are small things that don't matter much.
- Accept the things we can't change. The thing we *can* change is usually us.
- Keep strong faith; it moves mountains.
- When it's time to go, it's time to go.
- Grief is a real thing that has to happen, but life does have to be lived.
- We have to hold onto things with open hands.
- Life is ever changing and change is good.
- One day at a time.
- Say what you mean, mean what you say, but don't say it mean.
- Be kind.
- Be me.
- Love never fails.
- I'm not afraid of dying, it's all a part of life.

We have to fight hard to keep the right perspective. We can get sucked under by negativity when we don't fight against it. That's probably what I am usually doing: combating negativity by soaking up positivity. That may be the reason that I do that so much, because it's my purpose to connect people with positivity.

Here's a quick recap of all the connections I've made this year.

- I have continued to go to recovery meetings every week this year. It doesn't take up much of my life but it does keep me thinking correctly and handling situations with ease. It keeps me connected with folks that are working on themselves and being honest about things that are going on in their lives. It is important for me to be surrounded by people like that.
- Restoring the Foundation Ministry has taught us so much about ourselves and about ministering to others. That has also been a great tool for our Pier 7 Healing House. I will be forever grateful for the people we have met and the process that they offer.
- Communion with God Ministries has brought me so much wisdom together with the deeper healing that Father has brought us into. It has given me revelation and truth about things that I have always wondered about. CWG Ministries has taught me how to create my own meditations to Jesus and to Father, my creator and the creator of the Universe. I'm camping out at this one for a while and seeing how many courses I want to take. We can use many of the things that we have learned here at Pier 7 Healing House. Thanks Tina Pocernich for the referral, it has changed my life.
- My main take from TerriSavelle Foy, my cheerleader of dreams, has been my hour of power in the mornings. And it flows right along with my journaling, meditations, and the vision boards.
- The one mile walk on Youtube with Leslie Sansone, along with my Weight Watchers keeps me on track with

my weight. I am grateful that something as simple as these two things can keep me in line.
- Forty-four years of hairstyling has trained me to get along with people and take care of them. I love to have soft music playing in the salon to create a spa experience. This is what led me to creating the meditations. You will be able to find the meditations on YouTube and on our website.

I would like to introduce what Father has produced in my life to help me bloom and to help others bloom. He placed me with a husband that was designed perfectly for me. Our life experiences work together to bring healing and freedom to others. What we are doing together is fresh and new. It involves deep level healing along with recovery. The message that we have is unique. We believe that trauma has been in our life for a reason which includes experience to help others. We do not believe that divorce, abandonment, failure, lack, or abuse in our lives mean that we or anyone else can't be used by God.

Enough about us, what about you? What do you want and need in your life to help you move forward? Do you know your purpose? Don't let anything stop you or hold you back!

I just wanted to share my life and my heart with you. I sincerely hope that something I have said may have touched your life. If you ever need anything we are here. Please reach out to Pier 7 Healing House. Remember, it's harvest time!

16

"RESTORED TO BLOOM"

I started out so bright and shining,
Through many days so blissful and free.
Then trauma set in and dampened the bloom,
Many times too foggy to see.

Walking through life
The stormy weather came
So much opposition, digging up my roots
I would never be the same.

Swimming upstream
With joy all along the way.
With a broken heart
Waiting for a better day.

The fleeting better days would come
They'd water me and watch me grow
But that storm came along
And gave me a heavy blow.

The sun would shine and warm me up
I'd stretch up taller to the sky
I'd never stretched this tall before
But knocked down low, I thought I'd die.

The water from the rain came
The dirt plowed just right
I stood up taller and taller
I knew it wasn't by my might.

It all came together one day
It didn't happen in one big boom
The sun, the rain, the soil-without my might
And I was "Restored to Bloom!"

-Jill Rogers

ABOUT THE AUTHOR

After overcoming trauma, Jill Rogers and her husband, Marty, decided to use their gifts and experiences to bring healing and restoration into other people's lives. They are trained in Restoring the Foundations and run Pier 7 Healing House.

Find out more at: http://www.pier7healinghouse.com

RESOURCES

PIER 7 HEALING HOUSE:

- Website: www.pier7healinghouse.com
- Blog: www.jillsblogspot.com
- Email: jillspier7@gmail.com
- YouTube: Pier 7 Healing House

RECOMMENDED READING:

- Shift Happens: Turning Your Stumbling Blocks into Stepping Stones
- Shift Happens: Stepping Stones Devotional Finding the Freedom to Honor Others
- Fearless AuthorMindset Workbook by Christopher Moss

RESOURCES

- Unleashing Healing Through Spirit Born Emotions by Dr. Mark Virkler
- Dream It Pin It Live It by Terri Savelle Foy
- Memoirs of an Invisible Child (Hope in the Darkness Book 1) by Kelly Walk Hines

RECOMMENDED WEBSITES:

- Al Anon Family Groups: http://al-anon.org/
- Pier 7 Healing House YouTube channel: https://youtu.be/uL_ilYjFov4
- Restoring the Foundations Website: www.restoringthefoundations.org
- Weight Watchers: www.weightwatchers.com
- Walk a Mile YouTube videos by Leslie Sansone: https://youtu.be/EiJyfVk95g8

ALSO AVAILABLE:

Shift Happens: Turn Your Stumbling Blocks into Stepping Stones

Have you been stuck and can't seem to overcome trauma in your life? Do you keep trying but find yourself back at square one again?

Yes, you can renew your thinking and conquer many obstacles in your life, including rape, divorce, PTSD, addictions, even forgiveness. This book shows you how.
Available at Amazon.com

www.ingramcontent.com/pod-product-compliance
Lightning Source LLC
Chambersburg PA
CBHW051410290426
44108CB00015B/2234